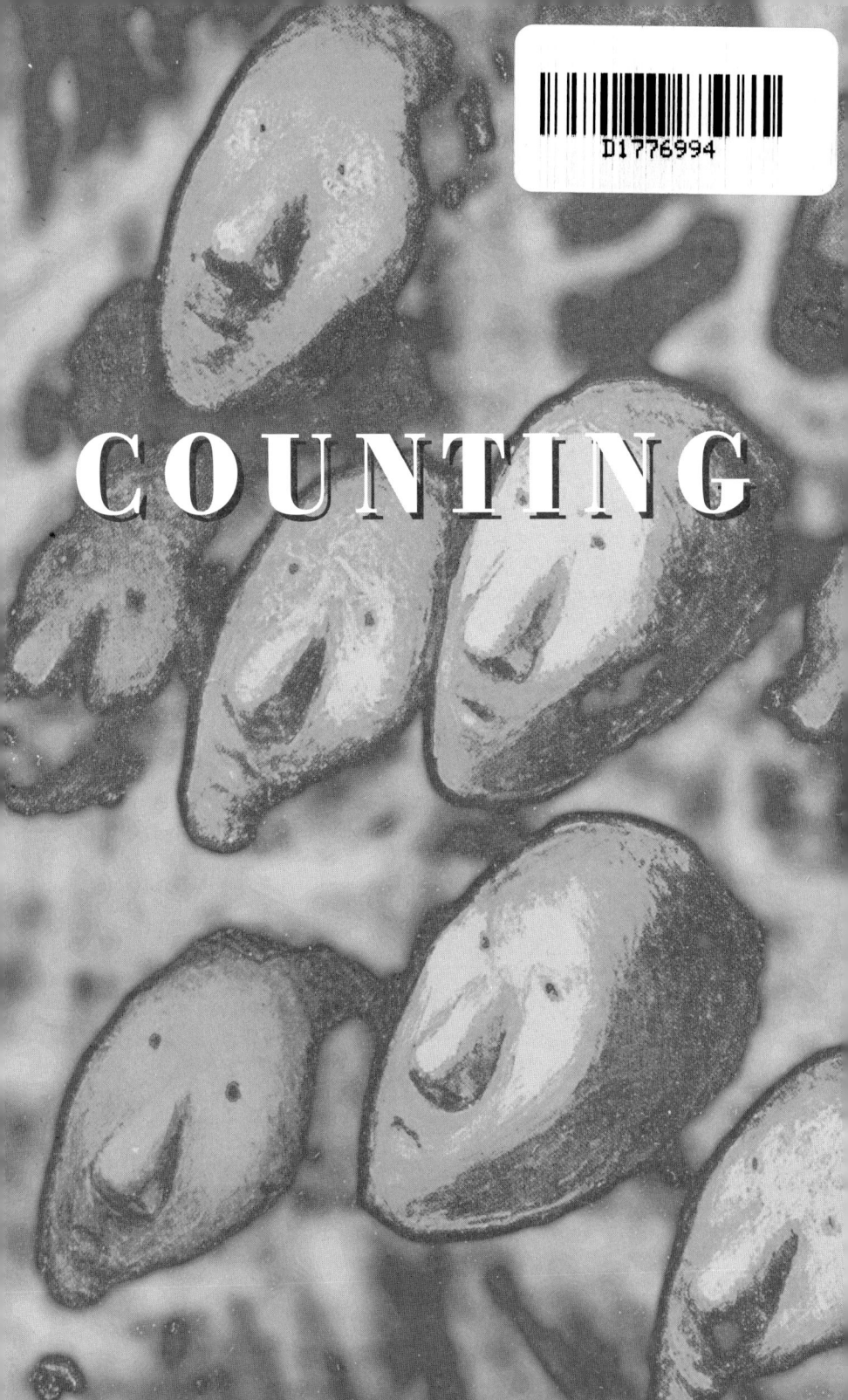

Dear Christina,
It was a real pleasure having you in my class.
Keep up the good writing
Enjoy

COUNTING

A long poem

Hilary Tham

CAPITAL COLLECTION
THE WORD WORKS
WASHINGTON, DC

First Edition.
First Printing.
Counting
Copyright © 2000 by Hilary Tham

Reproduction of any part of this book in any form or by any means, electronic or mechanical, including photocopying, must be with permission in writing from the publisher. Address inquiries to: The WORD WORKS, PO Box 42164, Washington, DC 20015.

Cover Art: "Reflection," acrylic, 27 x 37 cm., by Marta Levcheva

Book design, typography by Janice Olson
Interior art by Hilary Tham
Production management: Marta Levcheva
Printed in Bulgaria

Library of Congress Number: 99-75603
International Standard Book Number: 0-915380-45-5

Acknowledgements

The following poem segments have appeared, sometimes in an earlier version, in the following journals and anthologies to whose editors grateful acknowledgement is made.

Journals:

Atlanta Review: "My mother loved the bamboo tree" under title "Bamboo".
Minimus: "The Silence of Cats".
Waterways: "The loss of friendship" under title "Not Manderley"
Potomac Review: "Funeral Rites" retitled "At my father's funeral."
Storyboard: A Journal of Pacific Imagery: "We danced the bamboo dance" under title "Bamboo Dance".

Electronic magazine:

poetrymagazine.com/august/1999: "The mind goes where words can take us" and "The poem in the mind of the poet" together under title "Reaching the limits of language".

Anthologies:

Tilting the Continent: Southeast Asian American Literature, Editors: Shirley Geok-lin Lim and Cheng-Lok Chua, New Rivers Press, 2000: Under series title "Reflections", the poems "We come into the world with a cry", "Younger sister, death", "At thirteen I wanted" as "Teenagers are misunderstood as tadpoles". "The first time I saw Ronggeng", "When I was twenty I said", and "The world is a hard place".
WILL WORK FOR PEACE: New Political Poems, Editor: Brett Axel, Zeropanik Press, 1999: "It's not a perfect world, but" and "It's not a civilized world, but"

*This one is for Shoshana
with love*

Foreword

To Donald E. Herdeck for his support and mentoring of this book and for giving me good critical feedback from his perspective as a publisher, my grateful thanks. It was Donald who pushed me to write my previous book, *Lane with No Name: Memoirs and Poems of A Malaysian-Chinese Girlhood* (Lynne Rienner Publishers, Boulder, CO. 1997) with its focus the making of a poetic consciousness. As the founder and publisher of Three Continents Press until it was sold to Lynne Rienner Publishers in 1996, Donald published three of my earlier books and it was his suggestion that I write an epic poem of my voyage across religions and cultures, from Malaysian-Chinese Taoist to Asian-American Jewish, via Roman Catholicism and Existentialism that launched me on the writing of this book. Donald read this manuscript and wrote,

> "Each poem per se is good though I believe the three "USA" poems could be made one and tauter.... If your long poem, and parts of your many individual poems, are to be felt by your readers as confessional, as deeply sincere, as honest as you can make them, then these careful readers may come to believe you have too smoothly hopped and skipped from one lily pad to another without getting wet. In short, these show no pain, no struggle, no spiritual argument inside and outside your psyche. There must have been such, but there is no record as far as I can see in any of your poems."

I think Donald and I were after different things here. I do not think of myself as a confessional poet, and if I come across as hopping blithely from lily pad to pad, so be it. My changes in religion came as a process of maturation – I out-grew the childish world of Chinese gods who squabbled amongst themselves and needed to be appeased by bribes of food fests and new temples, into the Christian world of a God of Love who was paternalistic to humans. Then I went to college and wanted freedom from parental authority that dictated how and what I should think and do, rebelling against priestly authority backed by threat of Hell as punishment. After reading Sartre and Camus, I declared myself free of establishment religion and an agnostic, a hedonistic existentialist. Being twenty, healthy and single, I had no hostages to fortune. The only time I struggled and agonized (per Donald's definition and expectations) was the time before I agreed to convert to Judaism. Coming from a "hated immigrant race", the Chinese in Southeast Asia, I questioned the wisdom/sanity of my and my future children's becoming part of a more persecuted race, the Jews.

My husband Joe felt he would be betraying his Holocaust-decimated people into extinction if his children were not born and raised Jewish. I had no religion to offer and I recalled the warm security of a structured cosmology (albeit a mirror-world of Chinese society). America, with its Constitution of freedom of speech and freedom to worship, seemed a safe enough place to live Jewish. The modern Jewish concept of God seemed more like an artist-creator who, having created, gives his/her creations freedom to work things out for themselves, having left them a road map and detailed directions to find their way home in the writings of Moses.

In the early days, phrases like "God of our fathers" bothered me. It felt so patently a lie for me to say it. The Jewish God was not the god of my father or his forebears. Gradually, I came to believe that the Creator manifests in different forms to different peoples and that "God" (our human invented name for the Creator) was our inadequate, but necessary for us, need to name the spiritual source toward which we are all seeking to return. Once I arrived at this belief that our human languages were totally unable to describe the essence of God, the flawed words did not bother me any more. I do add "God of our fathers and mothers" to the prayer in our service for the Creator created both genders and, being perfect, cares equally for all of us.

In the prologue to my first book of poems, (*No Gods Today*, Kuala Lumpur, 1969) I wrote: "I will change as I will change as I grow older. I do not think I could write these poems again. They are the product of a certain stage in my life... I shall not come this way again." Those words apply to this later stage in my life. If my poems become fixed and unchanging, I will be dead. To live is to be ever changing, not like quicksilver, but like trees slow and steady and long in the shaping.

I wrote this long poem, now in bite-size segments, to share my thoughts and experiences (not to confess or invent agonies to fit the "expected view of conversions") and to celebrate the world I live in, the cultures that nourished my growth and the religions that are the mountain slopes I scrambled up, moving from ledge to ledge to stand where I stand now, looking about me, to say: "What a world! What a wonderful, imperfect world! And there is still more mountain to climb!"

With perfect thanks to all the writers, past and present, who have given me the world in their words.

Hilary Tham
May 2, 1999

Contents

Foreword 7
Counting 12

I. BEGINNINGS

The silence of cats 14
My mother loved the bamboo tree 15
Sometimes I think the metaphysical 15
We see eroded flesh 17
At thirteen, I wanted 18
We danced the bamboo dance 19
Younger sister, death 19
We come into the world with a cry 21
We judge gods 22
The first time I saw *ronggeng*— 23
My mother would not let me love her cat 23
At thirteen, I despised the unequal 24
Home is a place 25
In high school 25
The loss of friendship 26
How long do Zen masters 27
At twenty-four, I thought my future was fixed 28
I cannot marry a non-Jew, Joe said 28
A month before the wedding 29
Our wedding day 29
On our wedding day, the South China Sea 29
My mother insisted on Chinese 30
Leaving Malaysia 31
We flew to London and I learned I had never 31
London—Leicester Square, Piccadilly, Mayfair 32
London in Spring was freezing cold 32
Our budget honeymoon across Europe 33

II. EXPLORATIONS

On the boat leaving Greece	36
On the quay at Rhodes	36
In Tel Aviv, Rebbitzin Siegel	37
Rabbi Zuber	38
I did not feel Jewish those first years	39
After the Midrash class	40
I grew up believing silence	41
I look at my mother and see my future	42
Zen teachers say	43
When I am happy with you, I forget Zen	44
We begin with rain	45
We believe the past	46
A poem is never finished	47
White is the color of regret, not black	49
In the vet's waiting room	50
When a poor man eats a chicken, one	52
An unexamined life is a lost river	53
I often feel the need to hide behind silences	55
The first time I nursed my daughter, I knew	57
How my daughter Shoshana cried	57
We fail our children in many ways, in strange	58
Kindergarten age, Shoshana said	58
A February day, cold wind blowing	59
Shoshana, you still run tests to prove love	60

III. ARRIVALS AND DEPARTURES

Red is the color of action	62
The taste of chocolate, like faith	62
Are the multiple religions all impressions	64
The mind goes where words can	64
The poem in the mind of the poet	65
The Kabbalah says the Light we strive	66
When Moses came down the mountain	67
Light and life	68

Departing this body, this world	69
Bumper stickers are windbags huffing at strangers	70
The world is a hard place	71
Einstein said, God does not play dice	71
When my husband Joe is in Beijing	72
One summer, Joe took me sailing	73
Does a blind man know the wind	74
We have devalued love	75
When our dearest loves go	76
At my father's funeral	77
Chinese parents count on sons	80
The rabbis in the Sanhedrin said: A daughter	80
The world we make	81
A friend's daughter dies	82
I have seen how a potter uses all	83

IV. BLESSINGS

God in his wisdom gave us disposable bodies	86
It is better to light a candle than to curse	86
Let us bless, not curse, Eve	87
It's not a perfect world, but	88
Standing in the dark, seeing Orion's Belt	88
A gratitude for the present	90
A gratitude for children	91
A gratitude for poems	92
A gratitude for Joe	93
A gratitude for the body	94
A gratitude for America	95
A gratitude for the Creator	100
Notes	101
About the author	103
About the Capital Collection	104
About The Word Works	106

Counting

... what you give away/ is all that you own..... It's like counting leaves in a garden, along with the song-notes of partridges/ and crows.
        —Jelaluddin Rumi "Acts of Helplessness"

One: there were Chinese gods
sitting on altars
               wanting food
and temples with fish ponds.

Two: came Buddha wanting nothing.

Three: I found Jesus
    who was love and forgiveness after
      "Bless me, Father, for I have sinned..."

Four: were books that beckoned and I followed
    in half-lit rooms the shadows of Sartre
        and Camus' Stranger.

Five: I found lamps called poems,
    striking matches, rubbing words to make light.

Six: I met a light-bearer named Joe
    who asked me to convert
        to Judaism and I said, "What? You want me
to regress to man-made systems of worship?"

Seven: "For our children," he said. "Faith is
    the most comforting of security blankets."
Since God rested at seven, I did too.

I

BEGINNINGS

The silence of cats
before their feeding bowls,
like silent gods pondering
the failure of religion,
our two cats sit perfectly
still as Egyptian stone
statues, one gray, one black.
Their gazes pierce the air
above the empty bowls,
they miss their daily offerings.

The conjunction of cats, bowls,
emptiness and silence reminds
we have a moral contract
more binding than man-made laws:
to feed and adore them, they
to be themselves and everything
we attribute to them.

A cat's silence is pervasive
as incense as it sits after dinner
conning the essence
of linoleum by the back door.
Soon or late, a human is impelled
to open the door, hold it wide
while the cat yawns, sniffs
the night and decides he might
as well take a stroll since the door
is open, sure the world and we
will wait for his walking.
After dark, we too place ourselves
by a door and go confidently out into sleep
with the same careless assumption
that our housing will let us back in

on our return, that the world we know
waits for our waking.

՞

My mother loved the bamboo
                              tree
Bamboo has a thousand uses, she said.
Not one part is wasted. Bamboo shoots
are good to eat. We use the leaves
to wrap food. Old bamboo makes walls
and windows, tables and chairs for poor folk.
We have bamboo bridges, bamboo poles
for carrying burdens, to pick fruit on high trees,
to hang laundry out to dry. We weave young canes
into baskets to catch fish, to winnow rice.
And a young cane will beat the naughtiness
out of children.

Bamboo is what we are, she said. We bend
with the rain and the wind, we do not break.

՞

Sometimes I think the metaphysical
                                    world
a bamboo raft on which we stand
in tai chi trance, we stretch our arms,
this way and that, trying to feel
the wind's path, sense what wind knows.

We seek meaning
as we watch distant fires burn.
Looking for the future, we stumble

upon trap boxes from our past,
mothers with whom we never age
beyond childhood years, mothers
with whom we are forever thirteen,
all our experience, confidence
flee like kicked puppies from muddy boots.
We back into fathers who want their own
fathers back, hiding
their regret and their lack.
They will not turn the page
to see their own children grown
tall. They fix their eyes on what is gone.
They run their treadmill rounds, they
do not see what we've done, they
do not hear when we call their names.
They fix their eyes on what's gone, they
do not hear us call their names.
In time, we become our parents. Turn and look
at us, our children say as they grow
like rice, like corn, ripening in a row.
But we do not hear them, our skies
are dark with crows.

We see eroded flesh
                        and say
we do not want to die. We cry
when crying is permitted
until the age of three and then we learn
to show grace, we practice
wearing an inscrutable face,
the sanctioned mask of the race,

Each year at Ching Ming,[1] our parents
took us to visit the family graves.
We'd look at Grandfather's eyes, stern and serious,
in the lithographed photo on his tombstone,
and picture him horizontal in his coffin listening
to us, those eyes looking up through grain
of wood, blades of grass, at birds, unreachable sky.
"Be sure to visit our graves when we die,"
Mother would say as she set a feast:
sesame chicken, pork, rice, hard-boiled eggs and wine
for grandfather while we children hunted stones
to hold prayer papers in place on the grave mound.
We'd eat the eggs with tea, looking over the green hill,
the many humps of people sleeping
under the earth's grassy blanket.

We see eroded flesh and we ask, "Why?"

Our elders reply: Everyone dies. To live
is to struggle without cessation, as
the Yellow River floods with rain.

The nakedness of feelings
is discomfiting as nakedness of flesh
without skin, as horror of diseased gums

and genitalia.
Better to present a polite face,
not think about viscera or emotions.
We do the things we can—
the planting of grain,
the boiling of rice,
the filling of holes in stomachs.
There is no filling of holes in the heart.

5.

At thirteen, I wanted
                         to believe I was adopted,
to believe I could disown the family,
their voices and their needs.
I dreamed of a room of my own.

One night I stood in the dark and
thought about leaving home.
I stared until I was dizzy, gazing at stars.
I was nothing to them, not even a flicker
of a shadow on a leaf.
Somewhere a dog barked. And fell silent.
Only a frog in the weeds refused silence,
plaintively calling for a mate. A second frog
answered. And another. Soon the weeds were filled
with the multitudinous presence of frogs.

My mother had a story about the creation of frogs:
how a poor couple was buried alive in a mud slide.
A passing god heard their muffled calling—
"On," "Long": "Husband," "Wife,"
even as mud filled their ears, their mouths.
He gifted them with amphibian life,

changed them into frogs.

I listened to the frogs, their voices
telling a sad tale of mud, calling
to be heard, wanting to know someone
they loved was still there to love them.
Then I went in to my family.

We danced the bamboo dance
                                        as children,
skipping in and out, bare feet tapping
between clashing jaws of two poles sliding
inches above the ground. Tap-tap clash, tap-tap clash,
the two beaters grin fiendishly, the same grin I wore
when I took my turn as beater, rapping
and smacking the poles together.
I loved the pure physical beauty of dance,
knowing that practice was the key,
daring the dance again and again
until body knew its limits.
Dancers who refused to quit, limped for days
with crushed and swollen ankles.

Younger sister, death
                                    stalked you,
took you when you were three.
Mother would not say your name
out loud. Last year she spoke your name.
A Taoist told her you died because she
gave you a killing name, a name that called to death.

She named you *Plum Blossom*, forgot the sounds,
Choy and *Mui* also meant "brittle" and "decay."
Zen teachers say: "Everything is Zen.
The silence of birds when a tiger walks by,
the deer catching tiger scent,
the click of tiger teeth meeting in deer's throat,
the absence of hunger as tiger feeds, are Zen
and not Zen. Zen is Nothingness."
The student stares and longs for certainties, home.

Home is a place, with real things—hot rice,
beds to sleep in, shoes we remove
beside the front door to enter the house.
It is a place in the mind
where people were less kind than
we remember. Or kinder.
Memory is an erratic camera, with
variable film, and faulty zoom lens.
Memory is a telescope we view from both ends.

What I hold in my memory is a truth of you,
the three-year-old I knew, a cameo from the past,
withdrawn from time's revisions.
You wear, forever, rounded lips, soft hair,
wide eyes unchanged.
This is not the truth. Your truth was a stream
seeping through soil, around rocks, spreading,
reaching the thirst of trees and grass.

五.

We come into the world with a cry
                                             we protest
having to resume the burden of flesh.
We are recycled souls, Chinese elders say.
We return again and again to the Wheel, drink
the tea of Oblivion, forget we do not want
to dance the dance again.

Mother said she had been a man in a previous
life, a butcher with a bad temper,
said *The Book of Three Lives.*
In Ampang Temple, a Taoist nun
showed me my present life
in the book. A pen-and-ink drawing
of a Manchu scholar asleep
over his books. Great potential,
great laziness, she said.
She told me I was the wife
of a corrupt official in my past life,
said my future life was still blank.

I did not ask about my dead sister,
her third life, if she had been reborn.

I was held by Mother's net of cautions:
Do not ask after the dead.
Words have power, names have power.
Speaking the names of the dead draws them
back to you. Let the dead go to their futures.

What I carry from that day in that temple,
is the aftertaste of a lie—the lie I spat out,
when she said I should atone for my past
with donations to the temple.

卐

We judge gods
                     by their followers. What they do
in the name of their Almighty, we see
as attributes of that divinity, we follow
or turn away, seeking a perfect deity.

Persian poet Rumi[2] said, *"Ways of worshipping are not*
to be ranked as better or worse than one another./
Hindus do Hindu things./
The Dravidian Muslims in India do what they do./
It's all praise, and it's all right./...
Forget phraseology."

Rumi, Rumi, I want to agree, I who converted
to Judaism, word from Judah, meaning Praise God!
But bride burning is Hindus doing Hindu things,
treating women as property to be kept locked
is Muslims doing Muslim things. How
can the heart sing with such praise?

The first time I saw *ronggeng*—
the traditional dance of the Malays,
I wanted to stand and watch forever.

Ronggeng couples move as one,
their timing perfectly matched,
feet linked by invisible strings,
one stepping forward as the other
steps back, one advancing
as the other retreats,
almost touching, never touching,
always keeping a weave of air between.
How well the dancers *ronggeng*
depends
on how close to each
other they can come
without touching.

The words of the song tease:
"*Rasa Sayang*—The feel of love…"

5.

My mother would not let me love her cat
                                                said
"An over-petted, over-fed cat will catch no mice."
She did not pet her cat. She paid it a bonus,
steamed fish for each mouse it killed
and brought to her.
I do not have my mother's toughness.
My cats Misty and Merlin are over-petted
and over-fed. Lacking mice in our house,
they hunt out of doors, drag moles, birds,

once a squirrel to deposit at my back door.
I say, "Oh dear, poor bird. Good cat, good cat."

5.

At thirteen, I despised the unequal
struggling marriages in my home town, envied
the serenity of the nuns at school.
I wanted to be a nun.

At sixteen, I had learned *Te,* Virtue,
too well to abandon my parents as
they aged. Sitting on a curve of rain tree
root, I broke open seed pods, dry with ripeness,
picked out the red seeds. Threw them one by one
into the drain. They stayed where they landed.
No water flowed in the drain.
I remember the dry feel of dust
between my toes, and the light leaving
the sky, the road; road that ran forever
to where land touched sky. I remember
the crows overhead squawking, bidding
others settle down, quit rocking the branch.

Love is messy, life is messy, I told myself.
The product of love is life. The product
of life is love. Love which does not last.
Babies are delivered in a puddle of blood
and water. When we die, we leave our bodies
leaking for worms. I thought of hospitals
and delivery rooms and postal systems
and said: *We are God's mailing system; each birth
is a solicitation: "Please contribute... "*

I was more cheered by my cleverness than
the message, at the time.

⌗

Home is a place
　　　　　　　with a name
like Kelang, Arlington, Beijing,
Tel Aviv; a place with real things like
grass and dirt, soft furred cats, rough
bark on mimosa trees for cats
that love to climb trees. Home is a place
with real and invisible fences: Girls should
not climb trees or fly kites. Boys should not
play with dolls. Girls must stay indoors and
clean the house. Boys must marry and have sons,
to continue the family name and care of dead
ancestors. Girls must stay virgins
until they reach the marriage bed. How
I longed to step into a freer world, a larger future.

⌗

In high school
my friend Susan opened for me books
beyond the bounds of the Chinese world.
First sharer of wonder! First love, perhaps.
How bright the words on the page,
the mysteries of literature and myth,
the trail of others seeking meaning,
new thinking to us, how their words held
light like wind and sky to kites and the feathered soul.
I finally understood the ecstasy of monks
in their creation of illuminated manuscripts.

The world of the cloistered mind looked
at us, did not like what it saw. The nuns
took us aside separately, spoke long about
friendship, the wrong kind, sinful, eternal
punishment in hell's fires. The word "lesbian"
was never mentioned. "But Reverend Mother," I said,
"I would never do anything like that."

⌐

The loss of friendship
to time and distance is an enduring regret.
Fifteen years late, I flew to London to see Susan.
We were strangers in familiar faces,
filling blanks with polite talk of Shakespeare,
English soccer matches, pub brawls.

I do not see her face in dreams,
only places we have been. Once, on waking,
I wrote to her. *Last night I went back*
to your house in the old country. The orchids
were gone from your garden, only a rolling
swath of green grass where your dead father plodded
patiently after golf balls to sink them
into tuna cans. We had tea, your mother
elegant in gray hair and silk dress. She
was cool as the cucumber sandwiches
on the porcelain plate. She called me "Butcher"

and receded from me, the way people do
in dreams, the way you did, dropping years
between us as thorn seeds. I followed, losing
ground as grass became jungle, the wind
rattling briars, kudzu. I am left scratching

at omissions, guilt, a rash like poison ivy
in the blood, something for the enduring
until it too becomes past. The heart is slow
to learn it must cope with letting go.

I did not mail the letter.

5.

How long do Zen masters
                              live, I asked.
"The oldest was Master Pang," Mother said.
"He lived past nine hundred, but his mother
was pregnant with him for sixty years.
He was a graybeard when he was born."
Mother had many stories about Zen Master Pang.
When he was hungry, fish jumped
into his hand. Fish in his pan flipped over
to fry their uncooked sides for him.

How do you become a Zen master, I asked.
Mother said, "Zen is only a hair's separation
from madness. Leave it alone."

At twenty-four I thought my future was fixed

My college scholarship stipulated I would teach for the Malaysian government for five years.

At twenty-four, I visited a palmist.
Madame Katrivelu said I would have sons.
She said I would meet and marry
an economist, a man not of my race.
That I would live and die
in a foreign land. "Never!"
I said, thinking of economists
and men I knew.
It was a wise proverb that said, "Never call
a man fortunate until the moment he dies;
never name a man unlucky until he is dead." 3
Time bends and bends, hiding our future
until we turn the corner.

🔯

I cannot marry a non-Jew, Joe said

                                        troubled
by the duty laid on him by the Holocaust.
It is a need all living Jews hear and do not hear,
underlying their days and nights, ocean
breakers in the awareness of beachcombers, the
silenced roar of Jewish voices violently ended,
the thought: there but for the grace of God ...
my parents, I, would have been.
Joe said, "You must convert
so that our children will be Jewish.
I owe it to the memory of the six million."

🔯

A month before the wedding
                              I found a lump
in my breast. The doctor ordered a biopsy.
I said, "The wedding is off. You don't
want a wife with one breast."
"Of course I don't want a wife with one breast,"
Joe said. "But if it's a choice between a woman
with two breasts and you with one, I'll take you."
"Anyway," he said, "you're so flat-chested,
I'll hardly notice one is missing!"
Luckily, the tumor was benign and I
did not have to turn away from our future.

　　　　　　　囗

Our wedding day
                    Kuantan, February 16, 1971,
The Registrar of Marriages in the fishing town.
performed the ceremony. "Do you Hilary/Joe
understand that if you take another man/woman
for your husband/wife without divorcing this one,
you are liable to five years in jail and
up to one thousand dollars fine?"
"I do."
"I do."

　　　　　　　囗

On our wedding day, the South China Sea
was blue, Kuantan's beach sands were white
and fine where we sat.
Further down the coast, mangrove walked
flinging seeds into sea water to grow and
stretch into the unknown.

That night with Joe toasting marshmallows
on a driftwood fire on the beach, surrounded
by friends and the sound of ocean, I knew
if I looked away from the fire's dazzle,
if I waited for patchy clouds to clear, I would
see a universe filled with light

五.

My mother insisted on Chinese
ceremonies after the civil wedding.
She picked an "auspicious" day, had the tailor
sew me a pink silk cheongsam.
She made a feast and invited all the relatives.
"We must show we are not ashamed," she said,
"of you marrying a foreign devil."

On the auspicious day, we bowed before the family altar
offered tea to the household gods and dead ancestors.
We offered tea to Grandmother, seated ceremoniously
before the altar. She accepted her cup but sniffed loudly,
she disapproved of me taking a non-Chinese husband.

My parents accepted their cups but Father
was uncomfortable with Joe. The rest of the afternoon,
he spoke to Joe only to offer him more beer, fixed
in his belief that all white men loved to drink.
Older brother approved my marrying a Jew.
"Jews have a reputation for thrift," he said.
"With your spending habits, you need
a husband who can save money."

🖐

Leaving Malaysia
                    after our wedding, I
was not sad. I wanted to see Poets' Corner
in Westminster Abbey—the tombs of Eliot
and Auden; I would see Jerusalem—
Calvary, the way of the cross
where a rejected god once walked.
My mother wept, looking into a future
she could not see.
            When I came home to visit
the next year, she said, "Had I known
I'd see you within a year, I'd not have cried
so many tears when you left."

🖐

We flew to London and I learned I had never
known cold. I had grown up sweating
in tropical heat. I had not expected
freezing, or strange Cockney voices
whose English I could not unstring and
separate into meaning. Like a newborn
knowing only body temperature warmth,

I wanted to cry at the teeth-numbing cold.
That first morning staying with strangers,
friends of a friend of Joe's, who said they could
put us up for a day, I stood at the window,
shivered at rime frosting the pane.
I looked at Joe, a stranger with his eyes closed
in uncaring sleep, and I yearned for home,
warmth, the comfort of familiar things.

🔁

London—Leicester Square, Piccadilly, Mayfair
I had played Monopoly with these names.
London was Regent's Park and Baker Street.
London was the Tower and Traitors' Gate;
where the shades of Elizabeth Tudor,
Anne Boleyn, Sir Walter Raleigh stepped
out of wooden boats to climb worn stairs
into uncertain futures.
I knew London, knew its places
and flowers, whose names
I had loved all my life. Joe bought
me my first bouquet, a bunch of violets
from an Eliza Doolittle twin in Covent Garden
where we saw "Fiddler on the Roof."
When Chava sang: "Who could have known
that a man would come who would change
the shape of my dreams," she spoke
the poem in my heart, and I cried.

🔁

London in Spring was freezing cold
We huddled under heavy blankets, slept

with three pairs of socks on icy feet.
Looking at a jeweler's display—diamonds,
on a pair of black kid gloves,
I said, "Joe, I need to buy gloves."
You thought I wanted the expensive gloves
in the window. You said, "No, it's only
two more days. Paris will be warmer."

I had just made the connection:
gloves are not just objects in stories,
gloves keep hands warm.
I wanted any kind of gloves. I did not know
we were not talking about the same thing.

How threadbare I thought your love was, then;
how inadequate my cotton frock and jacket,
as we hurried from tourist sites, sighed
and thawed in the warmth
of the red double-decker buses.

5.

Our budget honeymoon across Europe
brought discoveries of bathroom etiquette.
In London, we learned to buy hot water
by the yard, "X" number per shilling as we bathed
and stopped, soaped, and stopped to feed
another coin into the meter.

In France, we puzzled over the bidet,
used it to wash feet.

In Zurich, we paid to obtain the key
to the bathroom with tub and shower.

You had always wanted to see Venice,
Venice that was sinking and sinks still.
How we loved its piazzas, its two
leaning bell towers, its crooked bridges
crossing dark canals, dark water
redolent with too much living
and *vaporetto* oil. I think we love Venice
with special urgency because the sea will take
her from us someday. There are days
we love each other with special urgency
because we remember death
will take us someday.

In Venice, you thought we had it made
when you found the door to the bath
open, only to find the faucets had no handles.
We paid our liras and the Madame produced
faucet knobs from her pockets.

In Europe we learned to take
nothing for granted. Everything
had a price.

II

EXPLORATIONS

On the boat leaving Greece
the purser asked, "You are married, please?"
We had bought the cheap passage, steerage—
separate quarters for men and women.
"It is early in the season. You are
the only passengers on this deck. Por favor,
will you consent to sharing one cabin?"
We were most happy to oblige.

The happiest times, soap bubbles, colorful
light in a drop of soapy water, vanish
behind the clutter of ordinary days.
For twenty-five years, I have not thought
of those three days on our cheap cruise to Haifa.

By day we had sun on the water, moon
at night. We had laughter. And groans
when we hit an elbow or head against iron
bed frame, squirming to fit
into the narrow bunk meant for one.
In the womb of the ship, below the waterline,
we learned by heart the geography of each other,
lingered like Marvell[4] over a curve of hip,
a breast, the texture of lips and skin.
Electrodes connecting to generate current,
we fused again and again, imprinted memory
of orgiastic pleasure on muscle and flesh.
Our bodies became keyed to each other's touch.

五.

On the quay at Rhodes
To see the future, you can look backwards.
A Chinese proverb says: The child of three

is the eighty-year-old. Genetic destinies
exist without our knowing: cells that divide,
multiply to form babies; that measure the lengths
of our lives, what will fall to bacteria in the air,
on our eyelashes and within us.

On the quay at Rhodes, looking up at the white
walls of the Crusaders' castle, you remembered
how you and your brother had played crusaders,
with sticks for swords and trash can lids for shields,
remembered how he would not play with others
even in playgroups and Kindergarten.
Later I would meet your brother Mike, find he had
replaced trash can lid with paranoia for his shield.

The next day the boat docked at Cyprus.
A man on the stony beach spoke to you
in Greek.
   You shook your head,
spread your empty hands,
       the way you do
each time Mike vanishes
       behind a false name,
to emerge in
   police stations, parole offices,
in the faces of
     vagrants we see on street corners,
to show you did not understand.

     ה.

In Tel Aviv, Rebbitzin Siegel
taught me Jewish prayers, how to keep a home
kosher, to serve a whole fish on Rosh Hashanah,

to give Joe the fish head so that he could say the blessing:
"May I always be the head of this house."
        Joe said she was a treasure.

Once Rebbitzin Siegel asked Joe an awkward question.
"How did you keep kosher in Malaysia?"
Luckily she came up with her own answer while Joe
was debating the cost of a lie. "Oh, yes, I remember,
you were in the Fisheries department. You ate fish!"
"Um, yes," Joe mumbled thankfully. "I ate a lot of fish."

Joe coached me in the Hebrew blessings.
He taught me to spit the Jewish way. I had trouble
pronouncing the "ch" in "Baruch." Joe said, "Make the sound
you make when you spit." So I said, "Ptui!" which is
the Chinese way of spitting, and not what he had meant at all.
We laughed so hard we did not finish our lesson that day.

ה.

Rabbi Zuber[5]
was a smiling kindness of a man, taking
pleasure in everything. On seeing us drive up,
he exclaimed: "Ah, it is good, you have a kosher car!"
At our puzzlement, he explained. "Your car
has separate seats, not a bench seat in the front."
How fortunate that the used car we'd bought,
without concern for *kashrut,* had bucket seats!
I heard again the voice of my teacher, Rebbitzin Siegel,
saying, "A woman must not offer to shake hands
with a man, she may not drink from the same cup or sleep
in the same bed as her husband when unclean
from menstrual blood. She should not delay
going to the *mikvah*[6] for purification afterwards,

for to deny her husband would be unkind."

"What is your reason for conversion?" Rabbi Zuber asked.
"So that my children will be Jewish."
"That is a good reason," he said. "If you had said, 'To marry your husband,' I would have to reject your application."

In the *mikvah,* in Elizabeth, New Jersey,
I immersed myself three times in flowing water.
Joe stayed with the three rabbis officiating
from behind a screen.
The *mikvah* attendant watched
to ensure not a single hair floated
on the water. After, Rabbi Zuber named me "Sarah,"
quoted Ezekiel, prophet who had wept
by the banks of Babylon.
With pure waters will I purify you and you will be pure.
A new heart will I give you and a new spirit will I put in you.
I will cause you to follow my teachings and you shall keep
my statutes, you shall be my people and I will be your God.

ש.

I did not feel Jewish those first years
after my conversion. I felt I was wearing
a new mask over old masks, I was dancing
a new dance, miming the moves. I felt a fraud
in synagogue, mouthing a lie when I said,
"God of our fathers." I wish I had known
what I know now: we are our memories.
I did not feel Jewish for I had no memories yet
of living Jewish, being Jewish.
The convert's mind
is a brand-new culvert that does not

know the feel of water until the doing
fills it with memory, floods it with rain.

ה.

After the Midrash[7] class
One wintry night, I drove Gloria home.
Her son had moved back with heavy luggage:
a messy divorce, a war over the children.
She said, "At the court hearings,
the lawyers cut open his heart like surgeons
looking for cancer. We cannot bear his pain,
only cope with our own."

She recalled a dream when she was pregnant
with this son. She was in her mother's house,
nursing her unborn baby.
Later, a friend asked, "How did you feel
in the dream nursing your baby?"

"I had felt nothing in the dream," Gloria said,
sitting in the car, unmoving as sorrow.
I looked at her house, rebuilt
after an electrical fire
left only the chimney, years ago.

"I realized then; memory is the womb
from which dreams come." Gloria turned the handle
on the car door. "I did not know then what I know
today, that the first time you suckle your baby,
a thousand cells rise in your body to pledge
allegiance to him, how fiercely you want to protect
your baby from everything that might hurt.
You cannot feel it until you feel it."

Time bends and hides the future. I watched
the streetlight shine on her thinning hair
as she trudged up the flagstone path, and hoped
I'd never have to be as valiant as Gloria.

5.

I grew up believing silence
was safest, that talk provoked attacks.
Malaysians still fear the dangers of free speech.
Though young Malays, Chinese and Indians,
have embraced computers, they talk
tentatively from the safety of screen names
on the Internet.
    I grew up knowing my skin
set me apart: Chinese, second-class citizen,
distrusted immigrant, money-grubber.
I learned early to avoid talk of politics,
Islam, the national religion. Everyone knew
police came in the night for the unquiet ones.
People vanished
and were said to have gone to Australia.
"Don't ask," Mother said.
"You'll have the police coming here."
In neighboring Thailand and Indonesia, the
immigrant Chinese camouflage themselves
in Thai and Indonesian names, feel safe
enough to protest the errors of government.
Malaysian Chinese keep their names and try to stay
unnoticed, like the Jews of Czarist Russia, hoping
that if they hugged the ground hard enough,
trouble would not find them.
Our parents said: "Stay behind walls,
walk with heads bent, we have all we need."
Meanwhile others grow tall

as we grow small
and then we're gone beyond speaking,
into a dirt hole below green grass
where worms blindly feast
unheard and unseen.

5.

I look at my mother and see my future
I see how time has marked its passage. I see
her loss of height, of hair, of bone from her bones.
My mother endures arthritis the way
the joists of old houses endure dry rot.
This same arthritis is encoded in my genes,
DNA that drives my joints and arteries.

Winter mornings I wake
with rheumatoid arthritis, to
fingers stiffened in sleep as if rehearsing
for their final positions. I have to rub them,

flex them, knead each swollen joint
before they will curl around a coffee mug,
lift and hold the waking brew.

I read in the paper that a study of vaccine
from white blood cells has found
cells from a patient's husband work
better than cells from strangers, which
are often rejected.
All the test patients were female.
Rheumatoid arthritis must be male,
prefers lodging with women.
Dr. Smith theorized that a woman's body
had become sensitized to the BLA molecules
on the surface of a spouse's cells
through sexual intercourse.

I say to Joe, "How strange that my molecules
should know yours, that my cells should open
for your cells?" He says, "Not strange at all,
after all these many years, these nine thousand
and eight hundred nights I've tried
to merge my cells with yours."

卐

Zen teachers say
The stillness of moonlight after rain
    is Zen.
The flight of the eagle after rain
    is Zen.
The nothingness, absence of feeling after pain
    is Zen.
The power to act and the wisdom

to know when to refrain from action
    is Zen.

Zen, pronounced Zhan in Cantonese,
my mother tongue, means three things—
achieving oneness with Nature and putting on power,
    the power of gods, the enduring hardness
    of mountains,
    the power to let go of worldly things, like water
    lets go of rock as it dives off a cliff and becomes
    waterfall.
Most Chinese gods were mortals who achieved Zen.

The second meaning of Zen is madness—
    the madness of a mind too small to contain
    the universe poured into it. It bursts
    and words and thoughts are dust particles
    spinning, colliding in a whirlwind.

The third meaning of Zen is lamentation—
    the mind that cannot hold the universe
    and loses it to avoid madness, yearns
after the Light and bewails the world still here.

When I am happy with you, I forget Zen
I take sunlight and safety for granted
I remember Venice, riding the train south
to Brindisi to board a boat to Greece,
but Memory has discarded most of that journey.
It gives me only the garrulous Neapolitan
salesman who insisted on showing you
the nude painted on the back of his silk tie.

I recall two things in Athens—moonlight
on the Acropolis, hot sun and dusty stones, ruins.
How could it be moonlight if there was hot sun?
I ask. Memory says, Oops, it must have been
sunlight. I remember the walk down the hill,
the blinding white of cobbled stone, the smell
of honeysuckle and bees droning
about the vine-draped walls. Did we talk
of ancient Greeks?

I like to think we talked of love, ours and
ancient lovers: Psyche wanting to know the true
face of Eros, Daphne running, changing
into a tree to escape unwanted love.
But Memory answers with a Zen nothingness.

5.

We begin with rain

When drought comes, the rice crop withers and dies...
The beginning of knowing is that rain is worth everything.
Kuan Yin, Goddess of Mercy[8]

We begin with rain and go looking
for relief for the soul's drought.
We know the end we seek
by different names:
Hindus say Brahman,
Moslems say Kavod (glory), al-Lah, (the Supreme);
Buddhists say Nirvana,
Christians say Paradise, Heaven, Jehovah, the Trinity, God;
and Jews say Shekinah, Adonai, Ein Sof (the Never Ending).

We seek return to the Creator using words
like oars pulling against the current.
We name the hoped-for joining:

Enlightenment, Zen, Zhan, Hebrew Ayin,
Moslem Ain, Nothingness, looking
for the unnamable. The heart's thirst
for loving, the mind's thirst for meaning,
the soul's thirst for its source-light, drive us
to take strange exits on the highway,
new paths in deep forests.

In Alaska's Drunken Forest, spruce trees
tilt and lean in every direction, their reaching
toward the sun unbalanced by permafrost
that thaws in summer, that leaves their roots
holding on to watery ice, shifting ground.

5.

We believe the past
is safe, the past is known
so we retreat and postpone
the future, where all is risk.
We pick up a familiar book and spend
recklessly of our remaining time
with old friends in old stories. Easier to cope
with faded pain , acceptable endings, known endings.
We insist on sleeping in our own beds
or else a two-star hotel room (three-star
is even better!) where we will get
what we expect. We harden with age, we dislike
the unknown, the unexpected. We refuse to change
habits, to contort our soul's contours to fit the
cluttered "guest room" in a friend's house.
We open invitations to dinners and parties
with foreboding, groan at having to prepare
a smiling face to meet the polite faces we will meet.
We wish we could stay home, in

our selectively furnished space. We wish
we could stay in our selectively furnished heads
undisturbed by strangers knocking on our gates.
They ignore our "No Solicitations" sign,
tell us we must show, with money, we care
about the dying of dolphins and the killing
of bacteria in our drinking water.

We have known the taste of lies
and grown accustomed to the taste.
We have learned to say No.
We have learned to be politely firm,
or rudely so, if that is what it takes
to make them go. They leave with a glance
that labels us ostriches with our heads in sand.
We grow weary of the calls
to care about this, *this* and that.

We have spent recklessly of the heart's coinage,
battled convictions to a draw; we want no more.
We keep our convictions safely penned
in our heads where they don't roll over,
politely play dead to please a friend.

ה.

A poem is never finished
only abandoned, poets say.
Poems feel unfinished, as
the un-voweled words in the Torah scroll.
We find new meanings as we change.
Poems are living things, like humans,
unfinished, incomplete. Poets know this
instinctively.

We go looking for completion, for a master
of the shadow world. We strain to see
the Source of Light behind the white gauze
screen where shadows dance. Seeking
the Maker of Universes, we feel our way
through shadows and make a song
to mark our passage.

Drink the wine, life's a grind.
This reel does not rewind.
Light a candle for the dead
Butterflies in the Creator's mind.

We bring nothing, we take nothing,
The joy of life is in the living.
We'll shed this body like a glove
Our only gift at birth is loving,

God's light is the soul in the mind.
Memory's the only gift soul leaves behind.
We move our wings, we move the air,
Butterflies in the Creator's mind.

White is the color of regret, not black
Don't tell a blind woman that.
I have been to two funerals this week.
I have sat in the synagogue, then followed
the hearse. I have watched a friend's coffin
winched down a hole.
I have sat in a church and seen an urn
that is the summation of a friend. Ashes
to ashes, thus to dust. I have seen
two friends buried this week.
In the length of time a world was made,
I have seen worlds unmade.

The people we love, they go from us.
The things we love, they fall away
from the compass of our eyes.
Our eyes cannot hold, our minds cannot
hold all that we would keep.
Our eyes fail, they cannot read
small print and we begin to dread
instruction manuals, complex procedures:
how to set up and operate a new TV,
how to make a computer run, retrieve, get mail.
Old dogs are hard to train. Old minds fumble
for an excuse, a reason why we do
not need this thing or that.

We sit in our dedicated armchairs, the ones
we've molded evening after evening to our shape.
We pet the dog, pick up the cat.

The cat rejects confinement on a lap.
He plunges a sharpened claw in our thigh
and we let go. We do not need that.

We go back into the past, the past is safe:
the pain there is second hand, something
we have known and endured.
Like the death of a cat.

5.

In the vet's waiting room
the men and women stand and wait.
They linger by the display of costly accouterments
for pets: catnip mice, hand-painted feeding bowls,
gourmet bird seed. They stroke the deluxe
condominium tree-houses
for felines, fake fur beds for canines.
They open their wallets and they buy.
They open their wallets and they pay
for manicures and real cures for the poodle,
the Great Dane, to gladden their barks or
alleviate their pain, stretch pet lives a month, a week.
They clench their teeth and jab needles into fur
to replicate failing kidney functions,
re-hydrate the animal. This they do
for a pet is family, not a mere animal.
"Wait," you want to say, "remember
that is not a human, that is a cat."

Our cats have personal and family names:
Misty Goldberg, Merlin Goldberg.
Vets insist on first and last names, they know
this fools our minds into acceptance and we'll pay
for physicals, dental care, surgery,
the best brand-name skills and pills
for our furred daughters, sons.

In the vet's waiting room, I am waiting
and ashamed: I am fretting about the bill
while Misty my cat is dying. I have seen
this same pinched look on faces waiting
in the pallid light of hospital rooms
while a father, mother, on life support
prolong dying in expensive ICU beds.
It is the look of animals caught in a trap.

America, you've lost the iron
in your soul. Steel with which men fought
for freedom, built bridges, made laws, made
differences between oppressor and victims,
not perfectly but as justly as they could.
Now we are plastic and PVC tubing, hollow
and malleable, Silly Putty in the clever
hands of super salespeople disguised as
TV evangelists, environmentalists, humanists, vets.
I am guilty, too.

I have bent with the wind. I have spent weeks
forcing antibiotics down my cat's throat,
irrigating his sutures a.m. and p.m.
After the injection that stops his heart,
that ends his pain, Misty's body will be cremated.
I am offered option plans A, B or C.
A: I can buy a burial plot in "Noah's Ark,
the local pet cemetery. The package comes with
funeral service and perpetual care of the grave.
B: I can receive his ashes in an urn
to keep or bury beneath a favorite rosebush.
Or C: he can be mass-cremated in distant fires
and mass buried with the ashes
of other pet bodies from vet freezers.

I pick option C—cheap only when
compared with options A and B.

I do not tell my mother this, my mother
who said when I wrapped her sick mouser
in a blanket, "A cat is an animal, not a person.
Don't mistake one for the other."

ק.

*When a poor man eats a chicken, one
of them is sick.* We chant mantras
of old knowledge, seeking definition
in an age of soft souls.

*For matzoth and a shroud, money
is always found.*[9]

*These three require guarding from demons
and liars: a mourner, an invalid, a child.*

*A person should not promise a child
something and not keep his word because
he thereby teaches the child to tell lies.*

*There are seven classes of thieves and
the first among them all is he who steals the mind
of his fellow creatures by lying words.*[10]

We would draw hardness into our souls
from the past, when people called things
by their names, not circumlocutions;
when black and white were not shades of gray,
when people were human and pets were animal;
when we were not afraid to name evil without
excusing it (she/he was abused as a child);
when we knew evil walked on two feet,

when "love" was a word never lightly used,
when people knew chicken soup nourished the body,
not the soul, and did not need to pretend
everybody was their friend.

We linger in the past, with people from the past,
when hearts raged out loud, not slithered
behind camouflage of politically correct diffidence.
When hearts knew words had power and
we cursed enemies with conviction.
Hot excrement in broken baskets for your mouths.
May your heads grow bald, may the wind
carry away your spices, may a blast disperse
your nail parings in the path of witches.

5.

An unexamined life is a lost river
It does not know its shape or
its effect on the stones it shapes
flowing over and around
and under them in darkness.

Your frequent traveling has sensitized me
to the absence and presence of joy
in ordinary things, eating breakfast
at the same table, curling into the curve
of your body as the rain beats a rhythm
on the roof, opening a book to look up
a verse in the Bible as we debate the ethics
of Lot offering his daughters to the mob.

We disagree on the freedoms
we allow our daughters.
You say they have too much of everything.
We forget to define terms of reference,
like our fight over gloves in London.

I agree when you say we have too much
clutter in the house. How did we come
to acquire so many possessions?
Water buffaloes are lead by their nose-strings,
humans by their desires.

Schopenhauer said our nature
constantly urges us toward satisfaction
of wants, of successive goals, none of which
provide permanent satisfaction.

We have not learned not to want,
only learned to resist the wanting,
to achieve equilibrium by balancing
one desire with another.

We resist buying a larger TV
with picture-in-picture. We have to save
for college education for our daughters.

I resist buying a better stereo,
orthopedic chairs that will not hurt
our backs. You do not like it when
you come home from China and find
the furniture changed.

5.

I often feel the need to hide behind silences
to keep hidden, and unnamed, denizens of my heart,
my heart's wild zoo. Walls protect the things within.
The things you do not name are not real, they
cannot hurt or be hurt.

When my first daughter was born, a friend asked,
"Did you count her toes and fingers?"
It's the first thing they do, many women tell me.
I have never thought of taking inventory.
The first time I hold my babies, words vanish
as hills from sight when the sun rises
above them. Touching the newness of her,
the love that grew as she grew from embryo to birth
finding outlet now, flowed between us, electric
connection of her miniature fingers curled
tightly around my finger.
With each baby, the same yet different beginning:
Ilana.   Shoshana.   Rebecca.
The only word I knew and said each time
was that baby's name. Fitting it on her,
wrapping it about her, again and again,
so she would know it, and know
the love for which it was code word,
belonged to her, and only her.

I have never named
the wordless terrors spawned
each time my child was threatened:
Shoshana by neonatal jaundice, Ilana by
non-normal parameters of bone growth at six,
Rebecca as a teen with friends who tried
to kill themselves in a miasma of depression.
The hard chrome terror of those days/nights
when nameless beasts shambled, howled,
slashing, clawing at the heart's walls, mind
refusing their names, scrabbling for words,
sending prayers without words
or addressee. *"Please ... please."*

And when time passed and the children safe
from presaged harm, how the shambling
shapeless beasts lay back down to sleep and
the heart's gates opened, unloosed wild horses
to run through sunlight flinging colors in rain,
fields of green grass dancing with wind and rain, the
quietly falling rain that washed the sky peaceful
blue again, empty save for the disintegrating
smoke of a jet plane to mark its passage.

The first time I nursed my daughter, I knew
how helpless I was to safeguard my child
from pain, from dangers hidden behind bends
in their lives.
                    Faith begins with acceptance
of physical limits, begins with humility,
submission to the will of the Creator.
It changes nothing, it changes everything.
It's that moment in tai chi where you ground
yourself, find your center of balance and harmony.
Nothing changes, but you feel centered now
on a bamboo raft borne on a rushing river,
you sense boulders hidden below water riffles.
It's that moment in tai chi when you are still
as a mountain, and you feel Time
moving
like a great river.

5.

How my daughter Shoshana cried
the first time she lost a friend,
when Natalie's family moved back to Utah.
She cried again, the second time she lost a friend,
a girl who liked the power of playing
with people's feelings. I watched her grow
a shell around her heart and remembered
the yearning of seashells, their memory of ocean.
echoing in their emptied chambers.

We fail our children in many ways, in strange
ways. Shoshana, at fifteen you asked me
for your baby clothes. I had given them away.

"How can you be so unsentimental?" you said.
You wanted the words of your lullaby.
I cannot recall the words of the song
I made up for you.
"You don't love me," you said in anger.
Your truth keeps out my truth: I love you,
have loved you from the first time you stirred
and turned in my womb.
You cannot feel love unless you believe it exists.
As long as you demand proof, you will not
feel loved, by me or another. You will only see
the things you look for. Disbelieving, you will find
signs you are not loved. Like the wind,
you cannot see love; you can only feel it.

5.

Kindergarten age Shoshana said
"I've been thinking about God.
God is the wind. You cannot see it,
you cannot hold it or touch it. You can
only feel it." You could be so wise
and so foolish: You collected injuries.
Real ones—with long waits in emergency rooms.
Less real ones—"Ilana got invited to more
birthday parties last year."

At Fenwick Island, you picked sea-shells
from the shore, all day, tireless, entranced
by the dance of wind and water.

When sunset poured light on the ocean,
you looked at the horizon and said,
"I want more!"

In fifth grade, you wanted to change your name
to a more popular one like Jennifer
or Katherine. You wanted a different
Hebrew name too. Being the only Shoshana
was a lonely thing.

The day you were born, you scratched your cheek
with a baby fingernail. Your sensitive skin scarred.
Twenty years later, a thin line still marks your face.

Shoshana, you are the daughter my heart
trembles for most, knowing you will receive
cuts from the world's sharp edges, scar more
than your sisters.

ש.

A February day, cold wind blowing
I sit on the college bleachers and watch you scrum,
ruck, tackle, bring girls down and rise with mud
coating your shirt. I am happy to watch
without fully understanding this sport,
this rugby you play, that
you call *"Elegant Violence."*
The game ends, but you do not
come off the playing field. "I'm
playing the next game too," you explain.
I pay the bills for emergency rooms,
orthopedic surgeons, buy you Ben Gay
ointment for aching muscles.

"February is my hardest month," you say.
"Not enough daylight, I get depressed.
I keep busy to get through it."

When it's not rugby season, you row out
on the Rappahannock with garbage bags
and friends to clean up the river.
You will make the world a better place
but you will not clean your room.
"Mom," you say, "I love you.
Leave my room alone."

כ.

Shoshana, you still run tests to prove love
You still test limits: of friends, love,
of my patience, my pocketbook.
You test yourself, you learned karate,
coached soccer, captained the rugby team.
I saw your axiom on a bumper sticker:
"If you are not the lead dog, the view
never changes."

Summers, you tested out jobs
in diverse trades; every place wanted you
to stay longer. Last summer, you went
to Israel, weeks of pre-dawn digging
for pottery shards, pieces of ancient lives.
I remember how you crawled to investigate
every room in our house.
You would not cease from exploration
even then. I hope the world will open
its doors for you. My blessing, love,
goes with you.

III

ARRIVALS AND DEPARTURES

Red is the color of action
White
is passive, the acted upon.
When we act, or are acted upon,
the object acted upon is pressured
out of its natural shape and forced
into another, repeated actions
force the object into deformity
or amorphism.

Soft souls do not act upon anyone,
not even their children, scrupulous in
their fear they might cause hurt.
The soft are acted upon by a harder
force, eventually, unable to hold, they lose
shape, they morph into ghost amoebae.

They become like a baby's words,
all vowels: "oo", "eee" and "eau,"
meaning escapes like water.

5.

The taste of chocolate, like faith
How can you describe the taste
of chocolate to one who has never
tasted chocolate? The truth of chocolate
can be known only by sucking it; the taste
is not to be found in words, but in the mouth
in the melting of butter, sugar, cocoa, milk
on the tongue and in the memory of
one who has eaten chocolate.

How can I describe my faith to another?
I could say it is this sense of nothingness
that nourishes the soul. This sense of
an inner world, concealed, a world that is not
our world, not perceived, not communicable.
I could say faith is a soap bubble
holding light.

We say Zen, or Enlightenment, or
Ayin, the word Jewish mystics use
for the human joining with the light of God.
Not God, only the shadow light that
emanates from holiness, the hollowness where
God was and now is not.

When we try to communicate the essence
of God, we reach the limits of language.
Words are inadequate as cupped hands to scoop sea
water, saying Ocean is salty, vast, deep,
Ocean is blue, green, turquoise,
aquamarine, all colors of light and dark.
The water in our hands leaks away, colorless.

I would be a hermit in a nunnery, tending the garden, contemplating the wind, emptying the mind to hear the silent music of the Unmusic = God.

garden
The fountain

Are the multiple religions all impressions
of the single truth? Wisdom wells up
in all languages, escapes
the netting of language, like the moon's
reflection in a pool. We cast nets spun from words
into darkness, we trawl for light,
debate the nature of God like physicists
arguing the nature of atoms and quarks,
before Einstein, before Stephen Hawking.

For comfort, I return to things I know,
an old Malay proverb: Water buffaloes are held
by nose-cords, humans by their words. And
its converse: Water buffaloes are led
by nose-strings, humans by words.

Until language fails us. Words fail us.
Like thimbles, they cannot contain the sea.
A million thimbles brimming with sea
water arrayed on a vast plain would still
not give us the reality of ocean.

〖5〗

The mind goes where words can
                               take us,
placing words like planks on quicksand,
stepping forward where word bridges hold.

The dead cannot bury the dead. The living will.
The living will tread where the dead have forged
a path, taking for granted the four-lane highways
spanning canyons, marshes where horses
once floundered and drowned.

The snake swallows the horse
and splits its skin, sheds its casing
    to contain it.
The mind takes in the world
and expands, sheds its casing
    to contain it.

The living walk on paths the dead have made
and marked with cast-off skins, casings of words.
The expanding universe knows not
its limits, has not reached the end
    of expansion.
The expanding mind knows not
the words for infinity. It only knows
it has passed beyond what it knows.

        5.

The poem in the mind of the poet
    is Nothingness.
The poem poured into vessels, words
    is Being.
Is Zen the nexus of the poem emerging
    from nothingness into being?
Does the sunflower know Zen, as it feels
the sun's rays, as it reaches toward light?

We spin in a metaphysic span of time,
We spin in a metaphysic span of mind.
We turn and turn, night-blooms toward moon,
seeking reflected light of the Creator.

Chinese mystics looked into night skies and said:
    "Nothing—the nameless
    is the beginning.

> *White Heaven, the mother*
> *is the creator of all things.*
> *All mysteries are Tao, and Heaven is their mother:*
> *She is the gateway and the womb-door."*[11]

The Sufi poet Ibn al-Arabi arrived at the same in Islam:[12]
> *"I was on that day when the Names were not,*
> *Nor any sign of existence endowed with name.*
> *By me Names and Named were brought to view*
> *On the day when there were not "I" and "we."*

Jewish Kabbalists say: The Mind in its casing (body)
is Being. The Mind expanding, out-reaching its casing,
is Nothingness (soul.) Being is in *No Thing Ness*
The mind is where the soul is, but it is not the soul.
Mystics arrive at the Unnamable, call it "Nothingness."
Following their tracks, we scratch our heads, we say
OOoom?

🔄

The Kabbalah[13] **says the Light we strive**
to reach is not God, *we dare not presume.*
It is light from the footprint of the Creator,
who has moved on after speaking
with Abraham, Moses, and the prophets.

Faith is the body sensing this sacred
nothingness hallowed by the Creator's
passing by. Faith is the infinite moment
of the big bang of the expanding soul,
the expanding mind.

The words of the prophets illumine
greatly for they were irradiated greatly.
In the precision language of physics, this
is process of luminescence: *when certain materials*
absorb various kinds of energy,
some of the energy may be emitted as light.
Incidental energy causes electrons in the absorbing
material to become excited and to jump
from inner orbits to their outer orbits.
When the electrons fall back to their original state,
a photon of light is emitted.
The light produced is almost always of lesser
energy than the origin of energy.[14]

Like phosphorescent mushrooms in a forest
illuminated briefly by a car's passing headlights,
we yearn for light, the passages of prophets.

ה.

When Moses came down the mountain
with the Ten Commandments, his face shone[15]
so brightly he took to wearing a veil.
In the forty years he talked with God, transcribing
God's intent into human symbols, Hebrew words,
he absorbed a miniscule amount of radiant light.

"And the children of Israel saw
the face of Moses, that the skin of Moses' face
sent forth beams; and Moses put the veil back
upon his face, until he went in
to speak with Him. (God)"[16]

Reading the Bible, I worry about God
being lonely. I think the closest God came
to friendship, was with Moses.
Moses, to whom He said, *"I know thee*
by name."
   Moses, the one prophet who was
familiar enough, or easy enough, with God's presence
to ask: *"Show me, I pray Thee, Thy Glory."*
And God said: *"Thou canst not see My face,*
for man shall not see Me and live ...
I will cover thee with My hand
until I have passed by. And I will take
away My hand, and then thou shalt
see My back."[17]
   A lonely thing, indeed—
being without equals.

ה.

Light and life
We use one word often for the other;
The only certainty we have: this light, this life
ends, will not last. So we go looking
for the moon in a pool of water.
The bereaved in the numbness of loss,
finds no place she or he can lean.

Grief comes out of nowhere,
and mourners turn their faces away.
Our friends lose their son in a car crash.

Dark, dark and empty now, the caves
that are their eyes.
We strike match after match,
rub words to kindle light in their eyes.
We watch as they turn hard and brittle, vines
shriveling from heat of the pyre.
We watch moon shrink
                         and tides turn;
clocks run down
                       and time take names, words
from our minds,
                       and we fall back
on hope, on trust, beyond questions.

We accept the nature of swans:
the trust of swans in water as they glide on
    the lake, their necks question marks
        asking nothing,
the trust of swans in wind as they unfurl
    wings and arrow their necks skyward,
the trust of swans, as water freezes
    under them, and winds turn white with snow,
    in their directional certainty of true South
        and kindly light.

ק.

Departing this body, this world
Kabbalists say, "The soul is filled
with the fullness of all the worlds,
the world above and the world below,
the world of our senses and the world beyond."[18]

The heads of the rabbis burst trying to comprehend this.

The soul in the body close to them says: "Headache?
Let me kiss it and make it better."

Seechō said, "Before you study Zen, mountains are
mountains and rivers are rivers; while you study Zen,
mountains are not mountains and rivers are no longer
rivers; but once you have had enlightenment, mountains
are mountains once more and rivers are again rivers."

人

Bumper stickers are windbags huffing at strangers
I stare at a bumper sticker that said: "I
believe in Random Acts of Kindness!" I know
the meanings for *random:* purposeless, haphazard,
without thought, meaning or intent. I asked myself:
Why would anyone do meaningless acts of kindness?
and thought of Maimonides who defined
eight levels of charity. The first level: to give
and be known to have given, the highest: to give
anonymously for job-training or capital
to start a business so that the needy will never
be in need again.

Yet any act of kindness, a dollar for a homeless
woman or the bearded panhandler who says he needs
money to get home for a son's funeral, to buy
a cup of coffee, has to be better than pretending
they do not exist. Each act of refusal petrifies
the heart. The hard shell we grow to protect it
turns prison, and the habit of loving departs,
as hermit crab abandons cramped shell
for more spacious housing.

The world is a hard place
it began with stone
pillars on a turtle's back[19]
and ends in stone
chiseled with our names;
Between the making
and the unmaking, flesh
and blood, bone and hair,
and then we, they are not there.
We look at our empty hands
and feel shadows and shade,
skin drying where water has been,
and are left with wind, know them
only by their absence. Water. Wind.

五.

Einstein said, God does not play dice
He believed the universe is orderly and never
random. He believed that Armageddon is
in our genetic code, said, "I do not know
with what weapons World War III will be fought, but
World War IV will be fought with sticks
and stones."

When the Atomic bomb blasted Hiroshima
and Nagasaki into nothingness, Einstein said,
"If only I had known this, I would have been a shoemaker,"
We ask: If we know the future, can we change it?
Can we change the future by changing ourselves?

Can a butterfly flitting from peony
to peony in Beijing cause a summer storm
in New York?[20] Can Chuang-Tzu dreaming

a butterfly cause a Tang empress[21] to regret
her ruthless road to power?

The heads of scholars burst trying
to comprehend this.

卐.

When my husband Joe is in Beijing
I know he is eating dinner as I read my morning news,
that he sleeps in China's night as I make lunch.
My mind accepts with ease that
elsewhere, people are raking
autumn leaves when newly leafed oaks
dust our cars with yellow pollen,
that December is summer
in the southern hemisphere.
Before the English discovered Australia,
before ships with wooden hulls and spars sailed
across the Equator, we would have said, "How
can winter be summer elsewhere. That kind of talk
is insane." To be sane is to resist
the nonexistent, hold on to real things.
It is easier to accept the coexistence of
'wheres' than 'whens.'

For us, the future is nonexistent, the future is
nothingness, as the past is
nothingness; memory, the rope bridge
we cast across a chasm, knowing there is no
ground on the other side of the valley of death,
knowing we cannot cross over, only stand
on precipice's edge, straining our eyes, see
distant movement of shadowy figures we believe

to be a beloved parent, lover, child.

How pleasant if we could believe Einstein, that
"The distinction between past, present and future
is only an illusion, however persistent," that
Time flows in both directions from us,
that the future exists simultaneously
with the past and the present, that

today, in New London, the snow is falling softly
as ski tourists emerge from supermarkets
clutching armfuls of groceries, that simultaneously,
Anne Boleyn is in the Tower of London, waiting
to lose her head, regrets or does not regret
having won the heart of a capricious king,
that simultaneously, my teenage daughter is smiling
at her first grandchild in a hospital not yet built.

5.

One summer, Joe took me sailing
It was an ordinary day, sunny on the lake.
Joe had just begun sailing, proud he had taught
himself. I was afraid he would capsize us.
I could hear the rush-brush of water resisting
the boat's passage, the thump-thump slap
as boat base met scalloping waves.
I dipped my hand in water, left it there
resisting water, for the feel of it, the sound of it.

Wind filled our sail and sped us across the lake,
through air, space, through time,
we left fear behind and launched into exaltation.
I opened my mouth to unloose a sound

that wanted to be born, knew in that moment
I was not a body leashed to gravity's collar.
I knew if I rose, I would sprout feathers,
      quills, pinions, wings to ride the wind.
If I fell, I would be fish in water, complete
      with gills and scales, fins and tail.
I did nothing. I stayed sane.

I have never told Joe this. Instead, I tell him
another truth: I am afraid of drowning.

5.

Does a blind man know the wind
has no color? That red is the color of
birth? Of judgment? Death?

We know what we know by our senses,
with a blind man's conviction that gold
has color, a deaf woman's trust that
there is music beyond air vibrating.
Our universe was mute
until the invention of radio caught

the hum of the universe,
static from the stars.

The world is what we know: concrete
and steel, skin and blood staying
safely behind skin.

Why is it that snow falling makes me silent?
That my ears mute the world's soundtrack
when someone I know dies.
Other senses
become acute, I can smell shadows, damp
earth, starlight on night grass. I sense
the shakiness of a bamboo raft
on a rushing river, the gravitational pull of black
holes when a loved one, No, say it, name it,
a Beloved, a more than merely loved,
a Better, Best sharer of the soul goes
beyond range of our physical sensing.

卐

We have devalued love

> *"If you love pizza, then marry it!"*
> Overheard at a children's picnic

These days, we use the word "love" like dollar bills:
we love mushroom pizza, my dog, my teddy bear,
that little black dress or your permanent hair.

We toss the word "love" like safflower oil on salads:
e-mail, thank-you notes, faxes for everyone we know,
We sign off with love to all, seldom "Sincerely"
 or "Truly"—social lying, unspoken
convention of our times.

When a love goes, we replace it from our broad
spectrum of democratized loves. One movie star
with another, one popular song with another.

This I know: I cannot watch videotapes
of Joe. The reels of him talking at seminars,
meetings, trigger alarms in me, warning:
that gesture of his hand, those crinkles
about his eyes when he smiles—they are all
I'll have when he dies. As if the alternate
future, the one without you, has arrived
before its time. I touch your still muscular arms,
pretend not to notice age freckles on your hand.
I will not mourn you before I must.

5.

When our dearest loves go
                                        we sit on low stools,
mourning stools. We touch the space, gape
at the exposed earth in our living room.
We call their names out loud, are answered
by silence from burnt out stars, dead
phone lines. Dreading future loss, we walk
in a dream of yesterdays.

Zen teachers say: Being is vessel that empties
and fills. Zen is nothingness that fills.
The stillness of moonlight on water
      pooling in a new dug grave,
the silence of mourners walking
      behind the hearse,
the numbness after the scorpion's sting,
the action of water on stone,

      the patience of water with stone,
      are Zen and not Zen.

Anesthetized, we do not feel the cut
of the knife, know it only by a thin line
etched red as blood escapes.

五

At my father's funeral
                      I am holding,
with my brothers and sisters, sticks of incense
before an eight by ten photograph,
our father in his early forties.
Behind the framed image, the real man,
the seventy-six years wasted body
is silent and still, his skin dull and
lifeless against the teak coffin's polished
glow, the sparkle of the glass-lid.

This is the third and final night
the Taoist priest chants sutras
lamor, lamor, lamor... to ease Father's
passage to the Chinese Underworld.
We place our joss-sticks in the urn
before the photograph; the priest's helper
places more in our hands. He tells us
to kneel, to burn joss-papers to placate
the spirits of roads and bridges, to protect
our father's soul as it journeys
through the land where no sun shines.

Last night, on the plane flying home,
I said Kaddish, read the Jewish service

for the dead. *Our days are as grass; we flourish
as a flower in the field. The wind passes over it
and it is gone, and no one can recognize
where it grew.* I mourned for my father,
knowing I mourned also for myself. I had
moved a generation, a row up
on Death's mulching schedule.

Tonight I am holding joss-sticks before a Chinese altar.
It does not matter, though my Rabbi will frown.
It does not matter—I know my father is not here.
I look at his picture, forty years young.
This was a man I never knew:
he was seldom home, busy always
with outside affairs, one mistress
after another, delicious dinners, laughing
with women, never my mother.

I am holding joss-sticks. Blue smoke
perfumes the air. It does not matter
though my Rabbi will shake his head.
He will mention graven images, false idols.
My father was my idol when I was young.
He was false to Mother and to us, though
he loved us perhaps, as much as he could,
being adopted and unloved by parents
who saw him as insurance for their old age
and afterlife, needing ancestor worship.
I loved him less than I could have,
admired him more than I should have.
It does not matter—dead is dead,
the man is gone, leaving old shirts
and shoes shaped by his feet, dusty books
and memories we sift, panning for gold.

He chose this photograph for his funeral,
wanted to be remembered young
And smiling. His heart was always
in its springtime while Mother's heart
grew bone-splinters, wanting more
than the boy-husband who saw her
as stern task-master to avoid and deceive.

In the house, she is overseeing the rituals,
the folding of silver paper into ingots
to fill twelve treasure-chests, the cooking
of food so his soul will not go hungry
on its journey west. She has bought
the best coffin, the best quality silk
burial suit, a Manchu lord's robe, cap
and shoes. She has ordered his favorite
sandals burnt with the paper mansion,
the red Mercedes of bamboo and paper,
the maid-servant with tea-tray, the man
servant with cigarettes and matches, all
art, paper and craft for the mirror world
his soul is wandering toward, having left
this house of his body, his 76 years.
She has not forgotten the years of long nights,
hot tears soaking her pillow as she aged alone,
waited for his return from another woman's bed.

Death does not erase the pain of betrayals;
it numbs to a bearable ache. Seeking meaning,
she says, "I must have oppressed him
in a previous life to have received such
sorrow from him. I hope the debt is paid
in full. I pray we do not meet ever again
in our future lives."

Chinese parents count on sons
to live with them, support them in their age, said
raising daughters to serve their husbands' families
was a waste of time and money.

Jewish sages discouraged dependence on one's young.
When a father supports his son, both laugh.
When a son supports his father, both cry. [22]

We return the way we came, turning
into our fathers and mothers as they turn
into children. They become unruly children
needing diapers.

America says "old
        is not acceptable."
America says "aging
        is not acceptable."
We call our old, seniors; put them away
in homes called "Sunrise," never names
that conjure endings, like "Sunset."
"Locust Grove" and "Bittersweet" are names
on homes from past generations when
people used euphemisms only with children.

司

The rabbis in the Sanhedrin [23] said: *A daughter*
is a vain treasure to her father. From anxiety
he does not sleep at night; lest she be seduced;
lest she does not find a husband;
lest she be childless; and when she is old—
lest she practice witchcraft.
In their time, parents did not fear

their children would put them in homes
where one is not dying, only
"Life-challenged," where the old are
deprived of freedoms, control
of their lives "for their own safety."

Their hearts burn to ashes, they know
they are diminished, powerless,
de-clawed indoor cats.

Unable to deal with the present, they retreat
into the past where the sun always shines and
they drive the Mustang from Baltimore to Boston,
see the road unroll forever before them, feel
the steering wheel quiver in their strong grip.

We pick up the pieces of our parents' lives,
unmatched dishes, books, and go on
with our own, string words between yesterdays
and tomorrows, knowing we must
be makers or we are unmade.

5.

The world we make
       is the place we live.
Home is a house on a low hill, a crow's flight
from Arlington Cemetery, green fields with mown
grass and white stones in neat rows, where dead
soldiers keep watch on Robert E. Lee's home,
used as army hospital in the Civil War.
I know the shapes of this landscape, the shapes
of its buildings, its trees, the curves of road,
the hidden trails that follow water down

to the Potomac. Flesh vanishes like last year's
grass but the act of one man can change a home
into a cemetery. Union General Montgomery Meigs
buried his son in Mrs. Robert E. Lee's rose garden and
began Arlington Cemetery, that the "renegade Lee"
should never be at ease in his home again.
Bodies of water, we change with each day we live.
The Potomac is not the same water.
Meigs' river is not our river.

                🏳.

A friend's daughter dies
and we look at our empty hands
barren, bare of words to help, to offer meaning
for their days that are now endless regret
of what might have been, done
or undone, said or unsaid.

The world's a slipstream flux of wind,
sunlight feels harsh as a father's anger
and teeth and mouths move

in a waterfall of white noise,
syllables looking for sense.
We come into the world with a cry, protest
the strangeness of air on skin.

Later, I learned the color of skin
that contains the self also drives us
into bondages, perceptions that fence us
in and fence us out. I have seen myself as alien
in another's eyes, been classified, boxed
and shelved, known myself diminished,
by that closed door act of labeling me
"yellow-skin."

Like the woman I encountered at MacDonald's,
when America took in post-Vietnam War refugees,
how she turned on me and my small daughters:
"You Vietnamese, you think you can come here
and take everything!"

Perhaps she had been wronged by one Asian.
There was no use in telling her I was Chinese,
that my six-year-old daughter had not meant
to swing out the car door against her car.
For her, we were yellow-skinned enemy, invading
her land, land she felt belonged to her by right
of Caucasian skin and light hair, forgetting
her ancestors, too, had been immigrants.

5.

I have seen how a potter uses all
the things that are in the earth, seen
how she begins with clay, shapes it,

fires it to bisque jar. She paints it with copper,
cobalt, silver glazes and fires it again.
At temperatures when liquids vaporize
and metals melt, clay holds
and hardens, purified.
I've seen a *raku* potter
transfer the fiery jar
to a lidded metal drum. She said
that as leaves, pine needles, newspapers
in the drum blaze into fire-storm,
oxygen rises to the glaze's surface,
drawn by fire's hunger, and is consumed.
This is the way she gets metallic sheens,
memory of flame, on the jar.
This is the way soul must feel, oxygen
drawn to fire, wanting light.

IV

BLESSINGS

God in his wisdom gave us disposable bodies
creating openings, arteries, glands and organs
all prone to blockage and malfunction, wear
and tear. As the years rise in our body odometers,
we see the light fail in the other's eyes,
know the unlucky one will be left
to close the lids of the one who goes first.
We see light grow in the children and raise
a glass to them, say, "This we did, this
we did well. *L'chaim!* To Life."
and wish them, "*Yasher ko'ah,*
May you go from strength
to strength." Our children look into their futures,
open roads that run forever
to where earth touches morning sky.

נ.

It is better to light a candle than to curse
the darkness, says an old Chinese proverb.
I say, let us bless, not curse, the darkness.
What would we do with unending light,
an endless day? Would we weep from weariness,
beg to lie down and rest. Or would we drift
the live long day, clouds in an endless sky,
doing nothing, feeling nothing?
Would we linger on the shore by a motionless
ocean, or bend to touch a pansy's petal
or laugh at finding the first snowdrop
in the dead grass of winter?
Would we drift past flowers without a glance
indifferent to their perpetual presence,
if they did not perish in the fall?
Would we look with longing at the stars?

Would we want to hold each other tight?
Would we cherish anything, love any one?

Let us bless the darkness that brings peace
after strife, rest after running, sleep
when the doing is done.

ה.

Let us bless, not curse, Eve
for eating that apple. Let us bless Adam
for choosing Eve over Eternity.

Bless Eve for causing darkness, endings
and beginnings. Bless Eve and Adam
for becoming parents, begetting children,
giving us heritage of flesh and fusion of flesh,
the joy of children.

Let us bless the Creator for being
duality, Light and Darkness,
Yang and Yin, Male and Female,
manifest in Adam and Eve.

Bless the Maker of Worlds
for making us darkness and light,
an ocean of contradictions.

A friend's daughter lives in fear. The court
will not order restraints on her stalker.
I pray for her as she appeals the case.
May God give her strength of heart and helping hands,
friends to guard her in time of need.
May God give the judge clarity

of perception to serve and mete out justice.
May God give the stalker freedom from his obsession
and dispel his malice. And may God give her light
and freedom to walk without fear all the days
and nights of her life.

○

It's not a perfect world, but
let us praise the Creator for delighting in gardens,
who grows Bahai gardens, Scientologist gardens,
Unitarian and Hindu gardens.
Bless the Creator for seeding gardens,
Zen gardens, Buddhist gardens,
Christian gardens, Jewish gardens,
Muslim gardens, all with boxwood mazes
promising a glorious center.

Bless the Creator who delights in wheat
and wild grasses, roses and purple loose-strife,
cacti and clover, and yarrow, who made
color-blind bees bring cross-pollination, color
to green flowers a zillion years ago.
Bless the Creator who rejoices in the living,
Who sorrows when His/Her creatures die,
Who rebuked the angels for rejoicing
when the Red Sea roared back into its channel
and the Egyptians and their horses drowned.

○

Standing in the dark, seeing Orion's Belt
listening to American frogs say "Ribbit, Bud – weiser,"
I ask myself: What if poets did not write

about death?
Would poems be forgotten
as helium balloons
that delight us a span and rise,
stringless, into sky?
Would we miss the stars, stars whose names
recall dead civilizations and their gods?

What if death did not exist? Would we
treasure the wisdom of the Greeks if they
were not ancient, merely old? Would we
take a trial subscription to their monthly journal?
Those Greek sagas make juicier reading than
the National Inquirer!

Would we need to make decisions?
Or commitments?
                      Shall I smell a rose?
Or write prose? Who will read it
when it's published?
                      Will publishers
take real instead of virtual centuries
to get that book into print?

Would we take our time, a decade or ten,
to reach a decision, another eon
to reconsider and reach another?
Would we smash our clocks, pause a hundred years
to contemplate a tree or a dog's bark?

I want to praise the breakable heart, biological
clock that makes us run, trying to beat the dark.

A gratitude for the present

Some days I grow fearful
of repeating myself in poems,
of repeating what has been thought
and said. I revert to the comfortable
habit of silences. Then I remember

how I loved Akira Kurosawa's film,
The Seven Samurai until I saw,
and loved more, *The Magnificent Seven*.[24]

I remember Steve McQueen as cowboy Vin,
telling the story of the man who leaped from a tall
building, how people on the twenty-second floor
heard him say, "So far, so good,"
as he plummeted past.
                         I wonder if
T. E. Lawrence thought, "So far, so good,"
before his motorbike rounded time's bend
into the accident that ended his life.

A friend's husband has left her, another
friend's husband has a brain tumor.
I look at my life and feel I have been most
blessed and I say, "So far, so good," knowing
death could be an eighteen-wheeler
roaring down the road
around the next bend in time.

A gratitude for children

A couple who did not believe in children
said, "To bring children into this world
so full of uncertainties, possible nuclear disasters
is irresponsible and a crime."

The laws of physics and motion hold true
for the energy of emotions. Love
that does not expand
                        reaches entropy
and shrinks into itself.
They did not remain married.

I am grateful for all my presents.
I am grateful for my pasts and the people in them.
I am grateful for my husband, for his love
And our joint belief in children.
May the Maker of Worlds bless our daughters,
each child so new, so different,
adding dimensions to our loving, our living.
May the Creator bless them, fill them with light
in their own galaxies, their expanding universes.

A gratitude for poems

The pink molded plastic train that was
penny whistle and first toy—how I loved
the pip-pip notes I blew with it.
Mother said I had to share it with Little Sister,
who promptly lost it.

When Little Sister died, I supposed I was sharing
her with unreasonable silent gods.
Later, I learned to let go of malicious gods.
I let go of Father's infidelities,
Mother's bitterness. I worked hard to make
my temporary flesh have meaning; to steep it
in integrity, honor, loving kindness.

This I know: the newborn calf does not fear
the tiger. I have learned to hold on loosely
to my children, knowing loss is in all futures,
that loss of life or loves may overtake us
in a casual mugging, chance gunshot, the
race riots I survived at twenty-two.
My parents never said they loved me, they and
I would have been embarrassed with such
un-Chinese behavior.

Marvell said, "The grave's a fine and private place,
but none, I think, do there embrace." [25]
I remember the grave is safe, the grave is full
of silences and I make a new poem.
I make a new poem and let it go.

A gratitude for Joe

When memory fails, it invents.
Joe remembers showing me Hoover Dam
when we were newly married.
I know I saw the Dam after we had children.
I know I saw it without him, with a tour group
while he was giving a seminar in Las Vegas.
How we argued, later accused memory
of failing in the other.

Now I am pleased his memory chose
to transpose my face on an old girlfriend,
that he sees my face when memory fails.

I will bless Joe for making me want
to come West. I will bless this West
where a man kisses his wife on leaving
the house and wants to kiss her again
on his return. Coming from the East,
where love is never spoken, hugging
and kissing are taboo, undignified,
where intimacy flowers and dies in dark
and silences, I want to bless this West
that believes in broadcast-sowing love,
showing tenderness, if only with hackneyed words,
Hallmark cards and advertised roses.

A gratitude for the body

The poet says, "The hand I placed on you, what if it
doesn't exist?"[26] Oh, you poet! What matters
is that at the moment of placement, the hand exists,
the body it touches exists.
Listen to hand's skin talking to body's skin,
what the body is saying to the hand. "Yes, yes...
here... and here, here now, there. Oh yes, more,
don't stop!"

Tomorrow or
another day, this hand may not be,
this body may not wish to be touched.

The world is a Pandora's box of interruptions,
diseases and viruses that cause
our drives to crash. Tomorrow
or the next day, this hand
may be crippled by arthritis, this body
may be riddled with pain and cancer.

Listen to hand's skin talking to body's skin,
what the body is saying to the hand. "Here!"
"Now!" "Yes!"

Accept the blessing of this life, this body, hand,
this hand on this body, the blessing of wanting
to touch and be touched.

A gratitude for America

Bless this America who believes
in a solution for every problem, from
computer dating for broken hearts
to healing stones, turquoise bracelets
for broken bones, who believes
in age-defying creams
and cabbage cures for cancer,
cloud seeding and weather charts,
infomercials and anti-stress tabs,
Novocain and Wal-Marts,
cordless phones, car loans and *carpe diem,*
seize the day, with credit cards.

Bless this America who has done away with
the Savings in Savings and Loans,
replaced them with ATMs, instant cash and
says, "How can I be overdrawn? I still
have checks in my checkbook."

Bless this America who has a fondness
for blondness, but bends backwards for the
African-American, Asian-American, the Apache
and the Pawnee, who assumes the burden for
the sins of our fathers.

Bless this America who wants grandchildren
yet believes in homosexual marriages
and alternate lifestyles, who hates lawyers
and loves lawsuits; this America
who believes in straightening everything,
from roads to crooked teeth to
crooked feet, and demands freedom with ramps,

motorized wheelchairs for crippled bodies.
Bless this America who believes
not in Judgment Day but in Mother's Day;
who believes in Jesus Christ and poltergeists
and the fair pricing system;
who believes in cookouts and Girl Scout cookies,
handouts and random acts of kindness,
Christmas lists and Toys 'R Us,
Liberty Bell and Tinkerbell.

Bless this America who rejected a king,
yet names its top of the line products "king," be it
beds, cigarettes, Nat Cole or Elvis.

Bless this America who believes in UFO's,
Elvis sightings, *Star Trek,* who believes in nuclear
power, electricity and efficiency,
yet adores all things made by hand: patchwork
quilts, lumpy candles and imperfect pots.

Bless this America who believes Nature
is a challenge to invent instant coffee,
instant tans with ultraviolet rays,
permanent press, deodorant sprays,
depilatory creams and hair growth Rogaine
internet sales and press-on nails.
I want to bless this America who believes we can
get anything anywhere with UPS, American Express.
Who believes in spare parts
for the body but not the toaster, says,
"Cheaper to get a new one."

I want to bless this ocean of contradictions, this
America who wears leather sneakers,

leather jackets, leather pants, yet
chastises others for wearing fur.

Bless this America who vanquished slavery
and forgets history, its young punching holes
in body parts to wear nose-rings, lip-rings,
slave symbols to show their free spirits.

Bless this America who believes in liberty,
equality and justice for all who want it
enough to start a campaign, and demonstrate
in Washington's blazing heat, freezing rain.

Bless this America whose women insist
on equality with the men, and have forgotten
how to sew to prove it.
I want to bless the women who insist men admire
their brains while their sisters buy silicone
breasts and low-cut dresses.

Bless this America who buys birdseed
for wild birds and is distressed the cat wants
to eat the mouse, who believes the underdog
does not have rabies, should be freed or at least
given a book contract to tell his/her story.

Puffing my cigarette, I bless this America
who believes it has changed smokers
into quitters by removing ashtrays
from buildings and airplanes.

Bless this America who laughs
at late-night comics' jokes on sins of our leaders

yet keeps voting them back into office.
Yes, bless this contradiction, America
who believes in self-improvement
and 'How To' books, scandal sheets,
square deals and used-car salesmen.

Yes, bless this duality, this America
who embraces refugees, sets up health clinics
and food stamps for them and wishes these
refugees had gone to Canada or Australia instead.

Bless this America who believes religion
should be a self-service mall; who invests
in pagers, car phones and answering machines
so as not to miss any call.

Bless this ocean of contradictions,
this America who believes in Free Speech
and the Gettysburg Address while pushing
political correctness and sensitivity training courses.
Yes, bless this America who rues violence and
loves martial arts movies, abhors killing
but insists on the right to bear arms.

Bless this America who tries to spread peace
and humane rights while exporting *Lethal Weapon*
movies One, Two, Three and Four.

Bless this humankind who tries
and tries, and gets up and tries again,
who believes the stars are within reach
of our grasp, soon as we invent
better cryogenics, star ships and vacuum shields.
Bless this humankind who believes the Universe

is a challenge to invent titanium hulls, moon domes
and terra-forming earth on airless planets.

Bless the Internet where the Web-wise
discuss differences of skin color and religion,
in hopes of promoting world peace,
where flames erupt as dialogues break down
and inflamed sensitivities demand
balm of appeasement, apologies.

Bless this humankind who has created
an epoxy that holds firm against the vacuum of space,
still puzzles over human drives, still seeking
to invent a bond that will hold
humans from hate, nations from war.

A gratitude for the Creator

Thank you, Maker of Worlds, for making us.
Thank you for the children of Eve and Adam
who will not cease from exploration, strapping on
rockets to go looking for God's other gardens.

Thank you for this Earth, with its nations that praise
God and human rights while hiding secrets behind walls.
Bless this civilization, growing at a snail's slow pace to us,
perhaps with the speed of time lapse photographs
to You who are the Master of Patience.

Praise to the Creator who loves gardens.
Praise the wild flowering of this world we know
for it will not last, it will pass into history
as ancient Greeks and Mayans did,
leaving seeds for another garden.

Praise this world and praise the Maker
for our presence in this garden.
Praise this hour and praise this dark
necessary earth that grows us.
In the beginning: *Now God saw all*
that God had made and here: it was
exceedingly good. [27]
The Source of Light sees us.
Sunflowers, we turn
toward the light.

Notes

1. Ching Ming: in the third lunar month, the Chinese visit the graves of family elders and offer food and prayer paper, Bank of Hell money, incense.
2. Jalal ad-Din Rumi (circa 1207 -1273) was the founder of the Sufi order, the Mawlawiyyah, known by their "whirling dervishes." From: Karen Armstrong: *A History of God, The 4000-Year Quest of Judaism, Christianity and Islam*, Ballantine Books, New York, 1991.
3. Sophocles: "Oedipus Rex." Also found as a Yiddish proverb.
4. Andrew Marvell poem: "To His Coy Mistress."
5. Rabbi Nathan Zuber of Roselle, New Jersey, was a Talmudic scholar who was acclaimed as a Rabbis' Rabbi.
6. Mikvah: the bathhouse for ritual purifying.
7. Midrash: intensive Rabbinic Bible commentary.
8. Martin Palmer & Jay Ramsay & Man-Ho Kwok: Kuan Yin: *Myths and Prophecies of the Chinese Goddess of Compassion*, Thorsons, London, 1995.
9. *Words Like Arrows: A Treasury of Yiddish Folk Sayings,* compiled by Shirley Kumove, Warner Books, New York, 1984.
10. A. Cohen: *Everyman's Talmud,* Schoken Books, New York, 1975.
11. *Tao Te Ching: The Way of Clear Virtue.*
12. Muid ad-Din ibn al-Arabi (1165 - 1240) often called Sheik al-Akbah, the Great Master.
13. Kabbalah: The book of Jewish mysticism.
14. Condensed from *Funk & Wagnall's Encyclopedia*: "luminescence" entry
15. Exodus XXXIV 29: *"Moses knew not that the skin on his face sent forth beams..."* The Hebrew word meaning "beams, rays or horns" was translated as "horns" in many texts and many artists, including Michelangelo, depicted Moses with two small horns among his curling locks of hair.
16. Exodus XXXIV 34.
17. Exodus XXXIII 17-23.
18. Daniel C. Matt: *The Essential Kabbalah, the Heart of Jewish Mysticism*, Castle Books, Edison, NJ 1995

19 In Chinese mythology, there are four stone pillars that hold up Heaven.
20 "The Butterfly Effect:" The notion that a butterfly stirring the air today in Beijing can transform a storm system next month in New York; from Chaos theory.
21 In the Tang dynasty, Imperial Concubine Wu seized the throne by poisoning the emperor and her son among others. Aging, she converted to Taoism and Buddhism, and had hundreds of statues of Buddha and bodhisattvas carved in cliff caves around Loyang, her capital.
22 *Words Like Arrows: A Treasury of Yiddish Folk Sayings,* compiled by Shirley Kumove, Warner Books, New York, 1984.
23 Sanhedrin: An assembly of Jewish sages in the Roman period (1st – 4th centuries CE). It was the ultimate authority on religious law.
24 John Sturges' film *The Magnificent Seven* was an American western remake of *The Seven Samurai.*
25 Andrew Marvell poem: "To His Coy Mistress."
26 Jorie Graham poem: "The Strangers."
27 Genesis 1.31.

About the Author

HILARY THAM, of Arlington, Virginia, is the author of five books of poetry, including *MEN & Other Strange Myths*, and a memoir, *Lane With No Name, Memoirs and Poems of a Malaysian-Chinese Girlhood*. Her work has appeared in such publications as *Antietam Review, International Quarterly* and in college texts. She has been a fellow at the Virginia Center for the Creative Arts and a winner in the Virginia Poetry Prizes. She holds a B.A. in English literature from the University of Malaya, Malaysia. Winner of ten Artist-in-Education grants from the Virginia Commission for the Arts, she teaches creative writing in schools and for the Writer's Center. Since 1994, she has been editor-in-chief for The Word Works and poetry editor for Potomac Review.

About the Artist

MARTA LEVCHEVA of Sofia, Bulgaria, graduated in 1985 from the National Academy of Fine Arts where she studied with the renowned Bulgarian artist, Ivan Kirkov. Her paintings have been featured in many collective and individual shows in Bulgaria, as well as in Washington, DC, and New York. She is the author of a collection of poetry entitled *A Portrait*.

About the Capital Collection

THE CAPITAL COLLECTION is a signature by the Word Works which features excellence in poetry from authors in the Greater Washington, DC area. The hallmark of this collection is that each book selected is financially supported by advance book sales and community contributions. The author also agrees to work with the press to promote the Capital Collection books, support other activities of the Word Works, and increase public interest in poetry. All inquiries must include a self-addressed stamped envelope.

The following individuals and organizations have contributed to the Capital Collection to make this book possible:

Patrons:

    Karren Alenier
    Mel Belin
    James Hopkins
    Miles David Moore

Donors:

    Myra Gondos
    Phyllis Green
    Reuben S. Horlick
    Laura & Jerry Jacobs
    Mrs. Pearl Koppelman
    Qun Li
    Judith McCombs
    Paul Napier
    Harold Novick
    Joe & Louise Pasini
    Arthur E. Reider
    Marilyn Shaw

Elizabeth Stevens
Lyvia Vivelo
George Young
S. Zimmet

Friends:

Susan Absher
Barri Armitage
Mr. Isidore Berg
Grace Cavalieri
Hana Hanbali & Usaid El-Hanbali
Carol Gallant
Jacqueline Jules
Marcia & Robert Kerchner
Mr. & Mrs. Joseph Kuney
Jacqueline Leder
Harold & Diane Mondschein
Fay Picardi
Helen Rebull
Lila Shapiro
Dr. Leo Sushner
Mr. & Mrs. Stephen Vilegi

Special thanks to the anonymous contributors who have generously supported this book.

About The Word Works

THE WORD WORKS, a nonprofit literary organization, publishes contemporary poetry in collectors' editions. Since 1981, the organization has sponsored the Washington Prize, an award of $1,500 to a living American poet. Each summer, The Word Works presents free poetry programs at the Joaquin Miller Cabin in Washington, DC's Rock Creek Park. Annually, two high school students debut at the Miller Cabin Series as winners of the Young Poets Competition.

Since The Word Works was founded in 1974, programs have included: "In the Shadow of the Capitol," a symposium and archival project on the African-American intellectual community in segregated Washington, DC; the Gunston Arts Center Poetry Series (including Ai, Carolyn Forché, Stanley Kunitz, Linda Pastan, among others); the Poet-Editor panel discussions at the Bethesda Writer's Center (including John Hollander, Maurice English, Anthony Hecht, Josephine Jacobsen, among others); Poet's Jam, a multi-arts program series featuring poetry in performance; a poetry workshop at the Center for Creative Non-Violence (CCNV) shelter; the Writers' Retreat workshops and readings in Tuscany; and Café Muse at Strathmore Hall Arts Center. In 1997 The Word Works collaborated with Mica Press (Ft. Collins, Colorado) to distribute Mica's Premiere Series of literary chapbooks.

Past grants have been awarded by the National Endowment for the Arts, the National Endowment for the Humanities, the DC Commission on the Arts and Humanities, the Witter Bynner Foundation, and others, including many generous private patrons.

The Word Works has contributed artistic and administrative materials to the Washington Writing Archive housed in The George Washington University Gelman Library.

Please enclose a self-addressed stamped envelope with all inquiries. Find out more about The Word Works at:

http://www.wordworksdc.com

email: editor@wordworksdc.com

Word Works Books

    Karren L. Alenier, *Wandering on the Outside*
    Karren L. Alenier, ed., *Whose Woods These Are*
    Karren L. Alenier, Hilary Tham, Miles David Moore, eds., *Winners: A Retrospective of the Washington Prize*
* Nathalie F. Anderson, *Following Fred Astaire*
    J. H. Beall, *Hickey, The Days...*
    Mel Belin, *Flesh That Was Chrysalis* (Capital Collection)
* Peter Blair, *Last Heat*
* John Bradley, *Love-In-Idleness*
    Christopher Bursk, ed., *Cool Fire*
    Grace Cavalieri, *Pinecrest Rest Haven* (Capital Collection)
    Moshe Dor, Barbara Goldberg, and Giora Leshem, eds. *The Stones Remember*
    Harrison Fisher, *Curtains for You*
    Isaac Goldberg, *Solomon Ibn Gabirol: A Bibliography of his Poems in Translation* (International Editions)
* Linda Lee Harper, *Toward Desire*
* Ann Rae Jonas, *A Diamond Is Hard But Not Tough*
    Vladimir Levchev, *Black Book of the Endangered Species* (International Editions)
* Elaine Magarrell, *Blameless Lives*
* Fred Marchant, *Tipping Point*
    James McEuen, *Snake Country* (Capital Collection)
* Barbara Moore, *Farewell to the Body*
    Miles David Moore, *The Bears of Paris* (Capital Collection)
* Jay Rogoff, *The Cutoff*
    Robert Sargent, *Aspects of a Southern Story*
    Robert Sargent, *A Woman From Memphis*
    M.A. Schaffner, *The Good Opinion of Squirrels* (Capital Collection)
* Enid Shomer, *Stalking the Florida Panther*
    Hilary Tham, *Bad Names for Women* (Capital Collection)
* Nancy White, *Sun, Moon, Salt*
* George Young, *Spinoza's Mouse*

    * Washington Prize winners

Requests for our brochure and other information must be accompanied by a self-addressed stamped envelope.